EMMA FARRARONS, a French illustrator and graphic
designer, is also the author of ~~the~~ Mindful ~~Coloring~~
Book. Born on the island ~~of~~ ~~Mauritius~~,
Emma grew ~~up~~ ~~in~~ ~~France~~.

She was trained in illustration at Brighton
College of Art and l'École nationale supérieure
des Arts Décoratifs. Having completed a textile
and printmaking course at Capellagården school
in Sweden, she has developed a particular love for
pattern and fabric print and is inspired by French,
Scandinavian, and Japanese design. She illustrates and
designs books, posters, and stationery.

When she is not drawing and designing, Emma enjoys
cooking, sewing, travel, and practicing mindfulness.
She lives in London with her Danish husband.

Share your creations using #MindfulColoring

See more of Emma's work at www.emmafarrarons.com

ALSO BY EMMA FARRARONS

The Mindfulness Coloring Book

A to Z of Style by Amy de la Haye,
illustrated by Emma Farrarons

London Colouring Book by Struan Reid,
illustrated by Emma Farrarons

THE MINDFULNESS COLORING BOOK

VOLUME TWO

THE EXPERIMENT

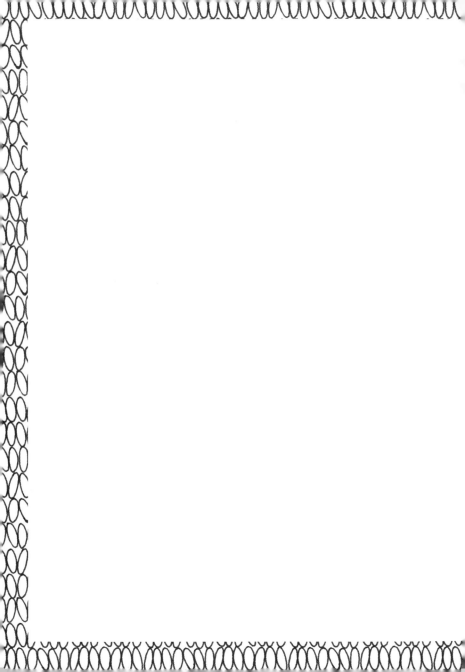

THE MINDFULNESS COLORING BOOK

VOLUME TWO

More Anti-Stress Art Therapy for Busy People

Emma Farrarons

THE EXPERIMENT

NEW YORK

THE MINDFULNESS COLORING BOOK—VOLUME TWO: *More Anti-Stress Art Therapy for Busy People*

Copyright © 2015 Emma Farrarons

First published in Great Britain as *More Mindfulness Colouring* in 2015 by Boxtree, an imprint of Pan Macmillan, a division of Macmillan Publishers Limited. This edition published by arrangement with Pan Macmillan.

The Experiment, LLC
220 East 23rd Street, Suite 301
New York, NY 10010-4674
www.theexperimentpublishing.com

The Experiment's books are available at special discounts when purchased in bulk for premiums and sales promotions as well as for fund-raising or educational use. For details, contact us at info@theexperimentpublishing.com.

Library of Congress Cataloging-in-Publication Data

Farrarons, Emma, author.
  The mindfulness coloring book, volume two : more anti-stress art therapy for busy people / Emma Farrarons.
    pages cm
  First published in Great Britain in 2015 by Boxtree, under title: More mindfulness colouring.
  ISBN 978-1-61519-302-8 (pbk.)
1. Coloring books. 2. Stress management--Miscellanea. I. Title.
  NC965.9.F372 2015
  741.023--dc23
                              2015033343

ISBN 978-1-61519-302-8

Cover design by Sarah Schneider
Cover illustrations by Emma Farrarons

Manufactured in the United States of America
Distributed by Workman Publishing Company, Inc.
Distributed simultaneously in Canada by Thomas Allen & Son Ltd.

First printing October 2015
10 9 8 7 6 5 4 3 2

For Cindy Chan

INTRODUCTION

Modern life can be very challenging at times. We rush around trying to get everything done: looking after our homes and families, keeping on top of our workloads, not to mention the seemingly never-ending texts, calls, and emails we receive throughout the day. Sometimes, even trying to make time to see our friends and enjoy our favorite pastimes can feel stressful. But we now know that taking a moment to pause and be mindful can dramatically improve our well-being, making us feel calmer, more at peace with our emotions and, as a result, more capable of dealing with the demands of the day.

Being mindful is about paying attention to the present moment, clearing your mind of distractions, and focusing on simply being. Pretty much any activity, done right, can be an exercise in mindfulness—sitting on the bus, brushing your teeth, or simply breathing in and out. But the act of coloring in—carefully and attentively filling a page with color, the feel of the pencil in your hand as you meditate on the beauty of the illustration—is particularly suited to mindful meditation.

This second book of mindfulness coloring provides the perfect opportunity to take a moment to be mindful. Let the intricate patterns and charming scenes inspire your creativity and relax your mind. Whatever you are doing, wherever you are, we hope you will enjoy taking the time to color in, de-stress, and be mindful.

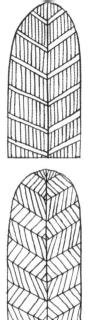

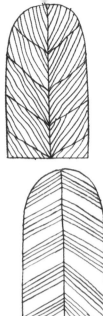

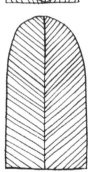
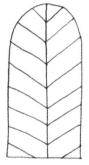

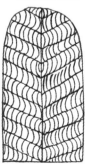
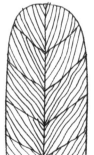
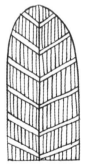

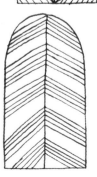

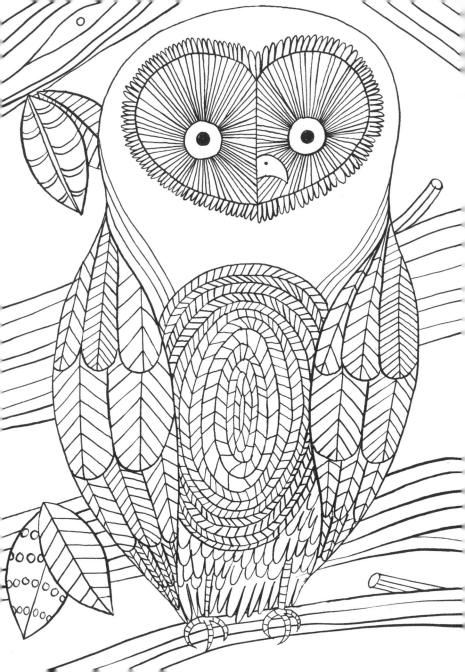

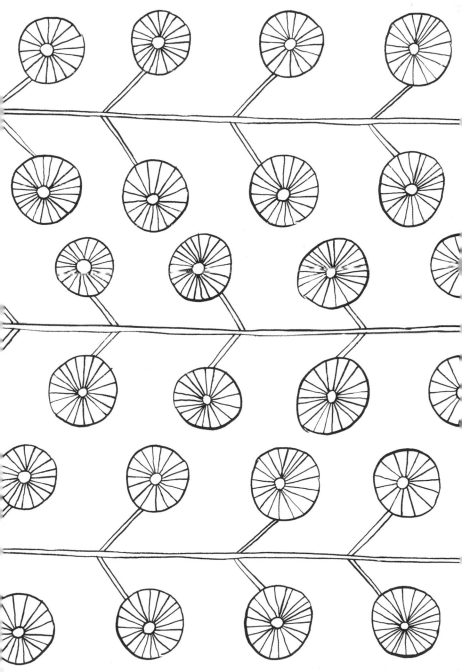

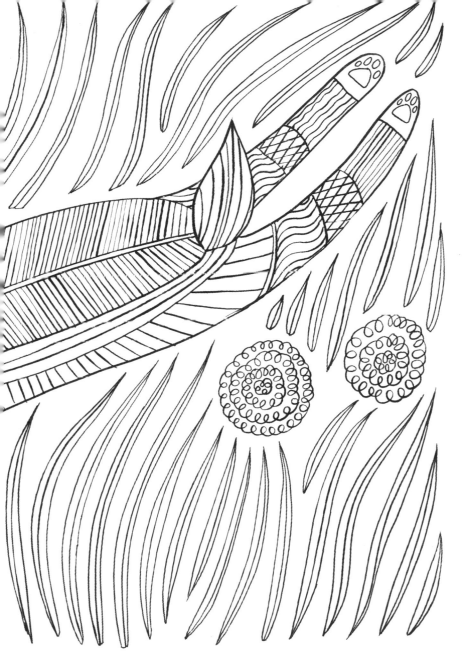

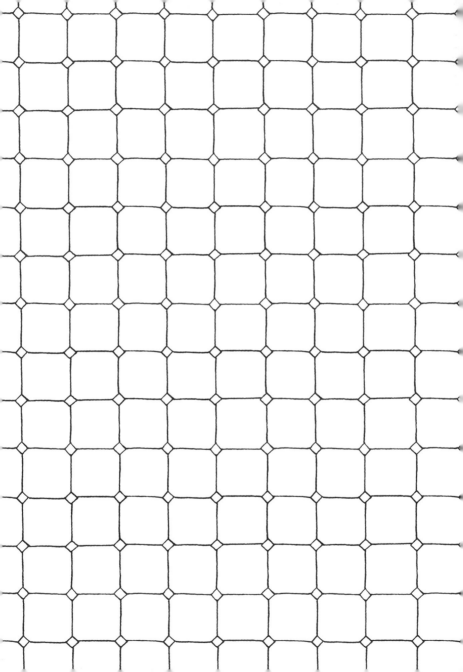

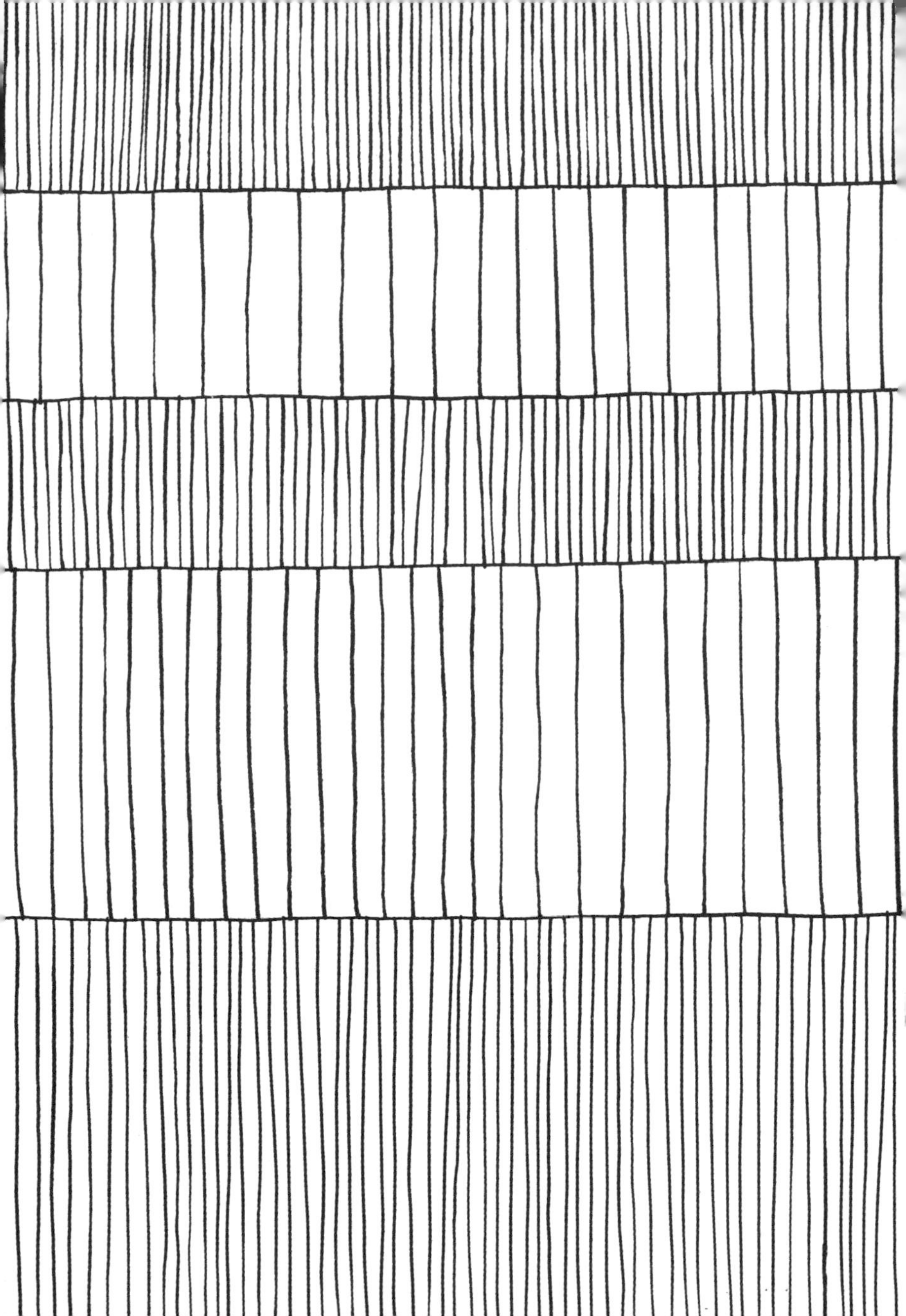

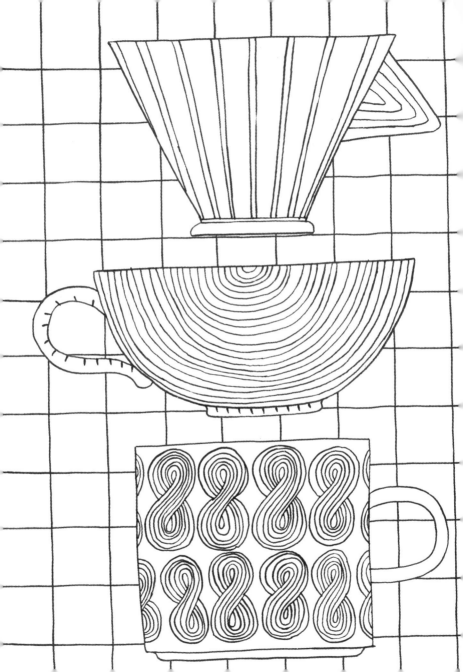

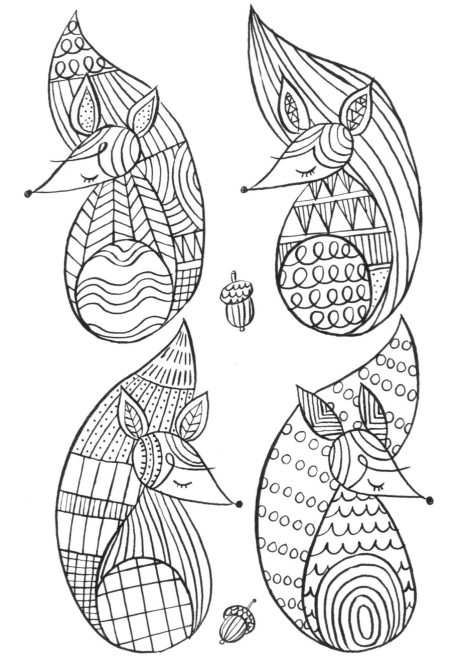

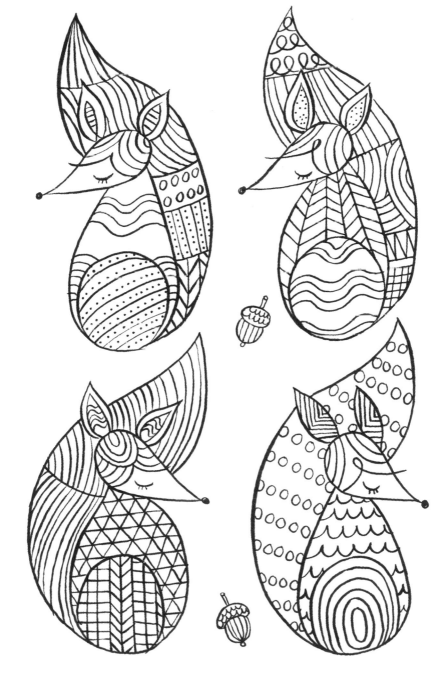

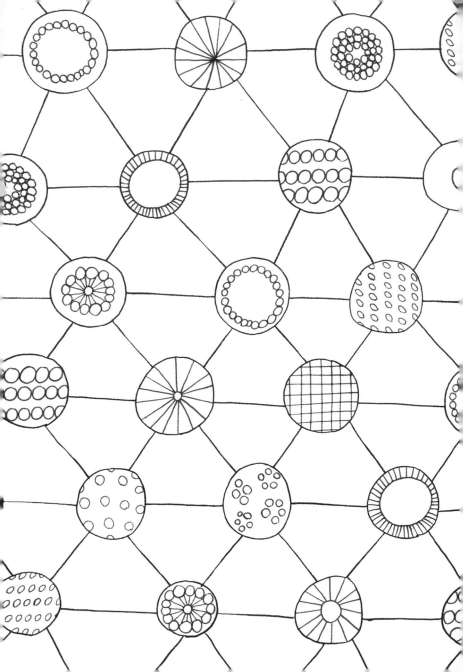

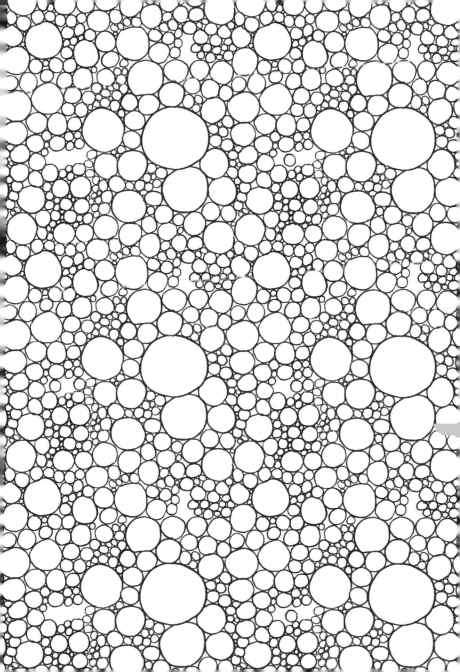

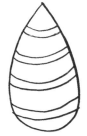

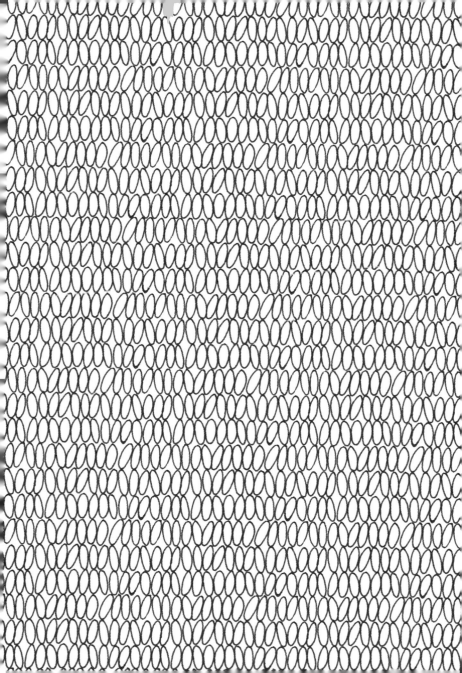

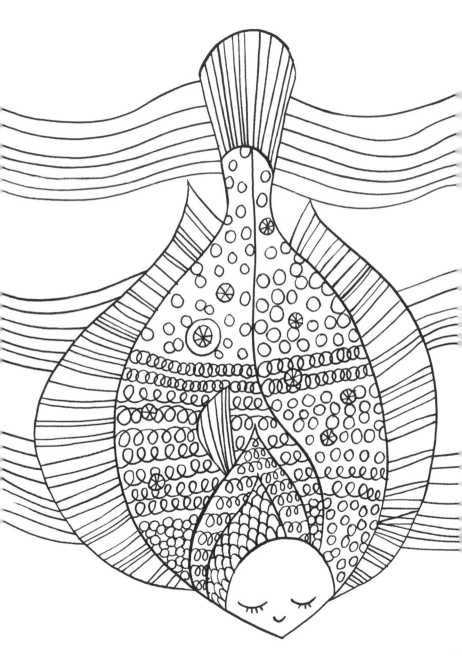

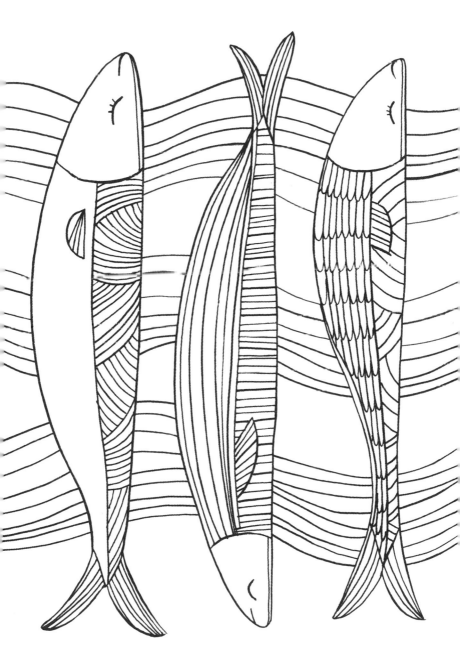

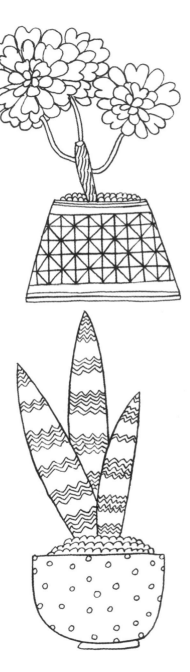

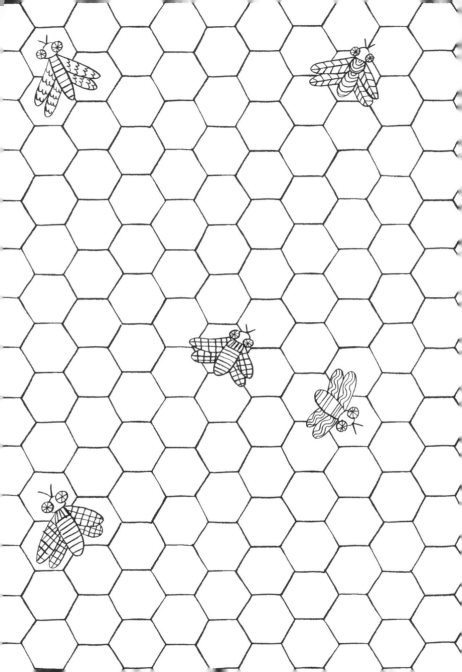

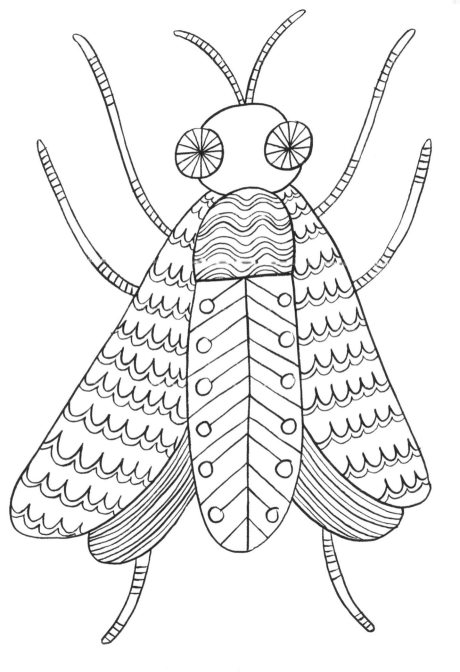

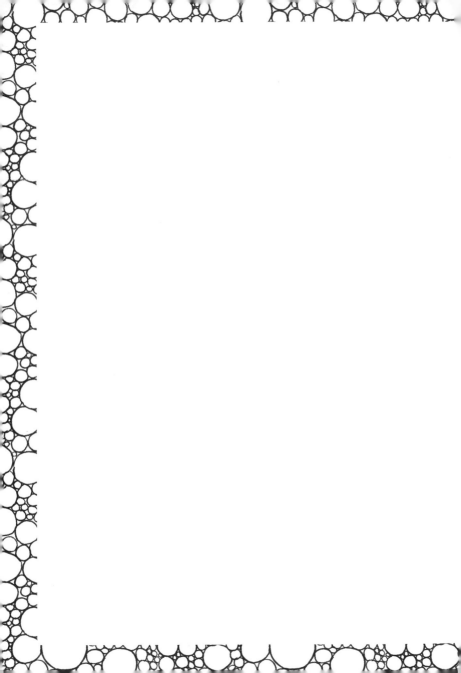

THANKS

I would like to thank Asger Bruun Jakobsen for cooking dinner for me those evenings I spent illustrating my mindful patterns.

A special thank you to my textile teacher, Lisa, for opening my eyes to the world of lines, pattern repeat, and the versatility of potato printing.

A big thank you to everyone who colored my first book.

EMMA FARRARONS
illustration & art direction

www.emmafarrarons.com